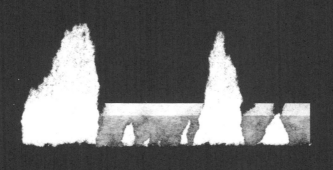

RON MILLER

THE SUN

WORLDS BEYOND

TWENTY-FIRST CENTURY BOOKS   BROOKFIELD, CONNECTICUT

Dedicated to Zachary Austin Miller

Illustrations by Ron Miller. Photographs courtesy of NASA.

Library of Congress Cataloging-in-Publication Data
Miller, Ron, 1947–
The sun / by Ron Miller ; [illustrations by Ron Miller].
p. cm. — (Worlds beyond)
Includes bibliographical references and index.
Summary: Presents information about the sun's origins, characteristics, future, and importance to the earth.
ISBN 0-7613-2355-4 (lib. bdg.)
1. Sun—Juvenile literature. [1. Sun.] I. Title.
QB521.5 .M55 2002   523.7—dc21   2001035811

Published by Twenty-First Century Books
A Division of The Millbrook Press, Inc.
2 Old New Milford Road
Brookfield, Connecticut 06804
www.millbrookpress.com

CONTENTS

Astronomical symbol for the Sun

A photograph of the Sun taken in red light reveals details that are not usually visible. [NASA/SOHO]

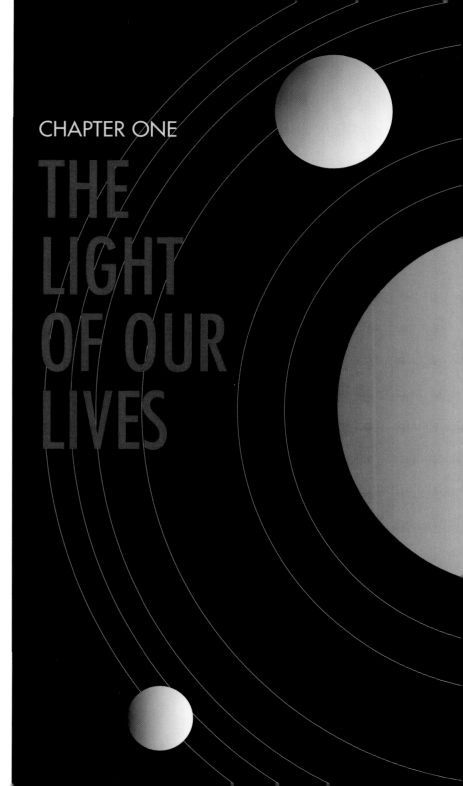

CHAPTER ONE

THE LIGHT OF OUR LIVES

All life on Earth depends on the Sun. All the **energy** we use every day comes from the Sun, either directly or indirectly. Plants grow because sunlight powers the process of **photosynthesis**, by which plants live. Humans then absorb this energy by eating plants or animals that have fed on plants. The Sun is the original source for the energy our bodies require.

We use electricity to light our homes, run our factories, and power our computers. To generate electricity we burn oil and coal—fossil fuels that come from prehistoric plants. In a very real sense, fossil fuels are stored solar energy. Even the power generated by hydroelectric plants comes from the Sun. The evaporation caused by heat from the Sun raises water from lakes and oceans. This water later falls over land and fills the reservoirs that feed great hydroelectric power plants. The seasons, the circulation of the **atmosphere**, the currents of the oceans, and the weather and climate are all directly linked to energy from the Sun.

Without the Sun, life on Earth would probably never have existed. It is hardly any wonder that many ancient peoples worshiped the Sun as a god. There were sun gods in the mythologies and religions of Native Americans, Phoenicians, Egyptians,

An ancient Egyptian depiction of the sun ship from the tomb of a pharaoh: The sun god is represented by a scarab beetle, helping guide the dead in their afterlife.

Mithras, the sun god of the ancient Persians

Chinese, African, and Oceanic peoples. The word *Sun* itself comes from the name of an ancient German sun goddess named Sunna. In nearly every ancient religion, the Sun was king of the day, representing the supreme creator of nature, light, life, and power.

The sun god was given different names by the many peoples who worshiped him or her. The Babylonian sun god, Shamash, was the bringer of light and justice. The ancient Greeks and Romans adopted many earlier gods into their religion, and they assigned the qualities of the Sun to their god Apollo. The Egyptians worshiped the triple solar deity of Horus (the rising Sun), Ra (the midday Sun), and Atmu (the setting Sun).

Ruins of temples to the Sun can be found all over the world: in Egypt, Syria, Rome, and elsewhere. The great monument at Stonehenge is an enormous solar calculator built by ancient druids to determine the arrival of the summer **solstice**, when the

Sun rises exactly over a special stone called the heelstone around June 22.

The Sun's predominance in ancient religions and mythology illustrates vividly the importance of the Sun to human life. Imagine the anxiety with which the earliest watchers of the sky waited for the reappearance of the Sun each day. Naturally, they wondered where it went during the long hours of night and wonderful stories were invented. For example, the Romans imagined that the golden-haired Apollo drove his gleaming chariot across the day sky and the Sun disappeared at sunset in a blaze of glory. Vulcan waited there with his barge to row Apollo across the night waters of the underworld, finally bringing him to the eastern gates of a new dawn.

A medieval representation of Helios, the Grecian sun god, in his glowing chariot

The Sun was one of the principal gods of many American Indian tribes. It is often associated with myths of the creation of the world. The Hopi of the American Southwest told this story:

In the beginning there were only two: Tawa, the sun god, and Spider Woman, the earth goddess. All the knowledge and power of the heavens belonged to Tawa, while the magic of the lower world was controlled by Spider Woman. Together they decided to create Earth between the heavens and the lower world. Tawa designed the features of Earth, while Spider Woman formed them from clay. Then Tawa invented the plants and animals, and Spider Woman formed them from the clay, too. When they were finished, they breathed life into their creations.

Now Tawa decided that there should be special creatures, resembling him and Spider Woman, who could take charge of the world and all its creatures. Again Spider Woman worked in her clay, creating these new beings. Again the gods breathed life into them. Spider Woman then summoned all the newly created people to follow her and she led them through the four great caverns of the underworld. Finally they came to an opening, which led to the brand-new Earth above.

Science Replaces Myth

The notion of the Sun as the center of the solar system goes back to the time of the ancient Greeks. The theory was difficult to prove and it went against both common sense and simple observation: It was obvious to everyone that the Sun went around Earth and that Earth was, consequently, in the middle of the entire universe.

The Greek scientist and philosopher Anaxagoras was banished from Athens around the year 434 B.C. for suggesting that the Sun was a white-hot stone no larger than the Peloponnesus, a peninsula of hardly more than 1,000 square miles (2,600 square kilometers). Earlier, people thought that the sky was a hard blue dome not very far above their heads, and that the Sun was a disk only 2 feet (0.6 meters) wide! While Anaxagoras' estimate was incorrect, his reasoning was perfectly sound. He had heard from travelers to the Upper Nile that the noon Sun was directly overhead in the city of Syene on the day of the summer solstice. On that day, a stick driven straight into the ground would cast no shadow.

Anaxagoras also knew that on the Nile delta, 500 miles (805 kilometers) north of Syene, the noon Sun on the same day was about 7 degrees from being directly overhead, so that a stick driven directly into the ground would cast a short shadow. He knew the distance between the two points and the two different angles. With this information, he calculated the distance to the Sun. Anaxagoras used sound logic, but he believed that Earth was flat, which threw his answer off wildly. He computed a distance of only 4,000 miles (6,437 km) to the Sun. Knowing this distance and how large the Sun appeared in the sky (about 0.5° wide), he calculated the Sun's width at about 35 miles (56 km).

More than two centuries later another Greek scientist, Eratosthenes, took the same basic data and came to an entirely different conclusion. He wondered if the difference in shadows was due to the curvature of a spherical Earth, rather than to the distance to the Sun. He used the data to calculate the size of Earth. His method was better but he came within only about 20 percent of the correct value because he didn't know the precise distance between Syene and the Nile delta.

A century later, new efforts were made to determine the size and distance of the Sun. Hipparchus, in the second century B.C., used the timing of solar and lunar **eclipses** to calculate that the Sun was probably at least 37 times farther away than the Moon and 12 times larger than Earth. Though he was off by 10 times on the distance and nearly 100,000 times on the size, Hipparchus was such a respected scientist that his figures were accepted for the following 1,700 years. It wasn't until the seventeenth century A.D. that the first accurate measurements of the Sun's size and distance were made. The methods used were very similar to those employed by Eratosthenes, but later astronomers had much more accurate data to work with.

The Center of the Universe

While scientists were attempting to discover the true size and distance of the Sun, only a few questioned the "fact" that the Sun revolved around Earth—and those few who suggested otherwise

MERCURY VENUS EARTH MARS JUPITER SATURN URANUS NEPTUNE PLUTO

A family portrait: the planets of our solar system shown to the same scale as the Sun

were never taken seriously. It was common sense that Earth remained in place as the Sun rose in the East and set in the West. This corresponded to religious ideas about Earth's role in the universe: It must rest in the center, while everything else—the Sun, the Moon, the stars, and planets—orbited around it. To doubt this seemed not only nonsensical but even heretical. It took three scientists studying more than 1,500 years after Hipparchus to finally set things straight.

The first scientist to question the established order was a Polish astronomer named Nicolaus Copernicus. Over a period of 30 years he worked out the details of a sun-centered solar system. His theory was published in 1543, when Copernicus was seventy years old. The aged astronomer died only a few hours after seeing the first printed copy.

Careful scientific observations were required before the new theory was accepted. A Danish astronomer named Tycho Brahe accomplished most of the work. For more than 20 years he carefully measured the movements of the planets. Brahe's observations led one of his assistants, Johannes Kepler, a mathematician, to the basic laws of planetary motion. These laws indicated that the planets must move around the Sun in vast elliptical orbits. But it still had to be proven that this was really so.

In 1610, the great Italian scientist Galileo Galilei was the first person to turn a telescope—which had recently been invented— toward the sky. He discovered that Venus exhibited phases just like the Moon, which proved that it must revolve around the Sun and not Earth. Finally, there was visual proof that Copernicus and Kepler were right: The Sun is the center of the solar system. We now know that the Sun is indeed very large, and that Earth circles it at a distance of some 93 million miles.

CHAPTER TWO

THE SUN IS BORN

It all started with a cloud. It was a vast billow of fine dust and gas—mostly **hydrogen**—billions of miles wide. Our galaxy was filled with millions upon millions of similar clouds, some smaller and some enormously larger.

A cloud like this is called a **nebula**, from the Latin word for "cloud." It is cold—around −279°F (−173°C)—and the cloud is thin. Most of space is a nearly perfect **vacuum**, with only one to five **atoms**—usually hydrogen—per .06 cubic inch (1 cubic centimeter). However, a cloud may have 10,000 atoms per cubic centimeter. While this is still nearly a vacuum—the air in the room around you contains more than 20 billion billion atoms in every cubic centimeter—the atoms are close enough together to collide and form **molecules**, or groups of connected atoms.

If the cloud is large enough—a few thousand times as massive as the Sun—and if it is not too hot, it slowly begins to collapse. Once the collapse starts, it cannot stop. The molecules start drifting toward the center of the cloud, where there is more material and the pull of gravity is greater. The moving molecules occasionally bump against others and create a little heat. As the cloud condenses, it grows warmer.

Deep within nebulae, dense knots of dust and gas form. It is in these nurseries that stars are born, as some of the knots become dense enough to begin to heat up.

What started the collapse? What gave the cloud that initial nudge? It could have been almost anything—perhaps the shock wave from a nearby exploding **star** (called a **supernova**) occurring in much the same way that a loud noise can start an avalanche. There is some evidence for this theory. Supernova explosions create huge quantities of radioactive elements, which would not be found in the original cloud. The solar system today contains a high concentration of these rare elements. This may indicate that a supernova started the collapse of the nebula that eventually produced our solar system.

The knot of condensing gas in a cloud is probably just a small part of a much larger cloud. The condensation begins where the gas is a bit denser than elsewhere. It's possible that at other places in the parent cloud, other small knots of condensing gas are also forming. Any of them may eventually become stars, too.

The center of the cloud, where the gas and dust is densest, grows warm then hot as more and more material falls into it. (If you've ever noticed a tire growing warmer as you inflate it, you've seen how a gas grows warmer as it is compressed.) As the center of the cloud becomes denser, its gravity becomes greater, and it pulls even more gas and dust into it. In just one year, a cloud of gas 2,000 billion miles (3,218 billion km) wide can collapse to only 200 million miles (322 million km)—ten thousand times smaller. Soon it becomes hot enough—more than 3,000°F (1,650°C)—to vaporize any solid grains of ice, dust, or even particles of metal. At the same time the **core** of the cloud grows even denser and hotter. Only a dim, reddish glow, like that of a hot coal, may be visible within the densely packed cloud.

(14)

Driven by increasing heat and pressure, the atoms in the core collide with tremendous violence. After perhaps only a few thousand years, the atoms collide so violently that they knock their **electrons** out of their orbits. This process, called **ionization**, occurs at a temperature of nearly 10,000°F (5,537°C). The gas, no longer composed of intact atoms, is composed of **ions**, also called **charged particles**. These are the electrons that have been knocked free, which are negatively charged, and the **nuclei**, which are positively charged.

As the cloud's core continues to heat up, the nuclei begin to collide. Normally, two positively charged particles would repel one another, like the north poles of a pair of magnets. However, the core reaches a temperature of 10 to 20 million°F (6 to 12 million°C), which forces the nuclei not only to collide but also to stick together. This is called **fusion**, which is a process that turns hydrogen into a new element—**helium**—that is twice as heavy as the original. Even more important than the creation of heavier nuclei from lighter ones is the release of energy in very large amounts.

It has taken our cloud 10 million years to contract enough for its core to reach the temperature needed for fusion to begin. The collapsing cloud of gas is a **protostar**. But as soon as the spark of fusion is lit, it becomes a full-fledged star. This new source of energy is so much more powerful than that created by simple gravitational collapse that the process of collapse actually stops. The cloud's outward pressure now balances the inward pressure.

This is how 4.5 billion years ago—50 million years after the original cloud of gas began to collapse—the star we call the Sun

As the knot of gas and dust collapses under its own gravity, the cloud begins to rotate and flatten. The center begins to glow as it grows denser.

As soon as the early Sun becomes dense enough and hot enough, fusion is triggered and a star is born.

Use a cup of coffee or a bowl of water and a spoon. Stir the liquid as randomly as you can—that is, avoid stirring in any one direction. Wait a moment and then put in a drop of cream or food coloring. Watch what happens. The swirls of cream or coloring will eventually begin rotating smoothly in one direction. No matter how much you try to stir the liquid, there will always be a little leftover motion that favors a particular direction. A nebula begins rotating in the same way.

1. Stir a cup of water rapidly in all directions, trying to make the motion as random as possible.

2. Place a drop of food coloring or ink into the center of the water.

3. The ink will begin swirling in one direction or the other. Compare the form the coloring makes to the shape of the Milky Way galaxy (page 23).

was born. The force of the Sun's radiation not only stopped the collapse of the star, it blew away most of the remaining dust and gas, except for a dense ring of dust that formed in the plane of the Sun's equator. But how did this ring of dust get there?

Ring around the Sun

When the original cloud began to collapse, its atoms were moving randomly in all directions. Soon, however, more atoms began moving in one direction than in another. Some atoms always moved in the same direction even though the rest moved in many different directions. Eventually the whole cloud started rotating.

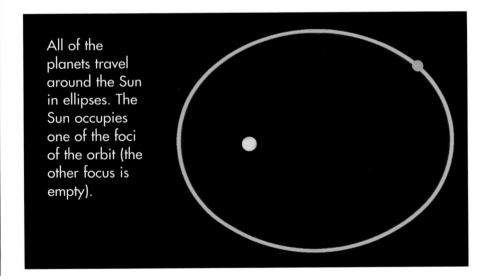

All of the planets travel around the Sun in ellipses. The Sun occupies one of the foci of the orbit (the other focus is empty).

As the cloud shrank it began to rotate faster. You have probably seen figure skaters spin faster as they draw their arms closer to their body. In exactly the same way, the cloud spun faster as it got more compact. The **centrifugal force** created by the spinning caused the cloud to flatten out. At first it looked something like a hamburger bun, but eventually it flattened out into a broad disk, like a CD, with the Sun in the center. This material, left over from the creation of the Sun, eventually became the planets—and is why the planets all rotate in the same plane and in the same direction.

The Sun has changed very little since it was formed 4.5 billion years ago. When it was young, it was a little smaller, a little fainter, and a little cooler than it is today. It became hotter for a short time and then slightly cooled off. Today it is 10,000°F (5,500°C), about 200°F (93°C) hotter than it was at its birth. Our Sun is a normal, steady, entirely average star known as a **yellow dwarf**. It's in middle age today, having gone through about half of its hydrogen fuel. It has about 6.5 billion years of life remaining.

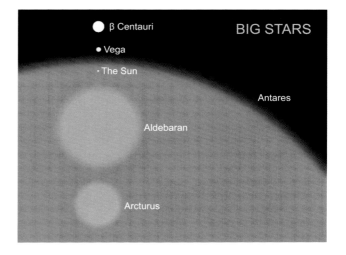

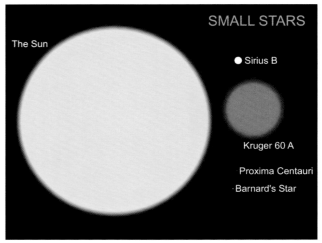

The Sun compared to larger stars (top) and smaller stars (bottom)

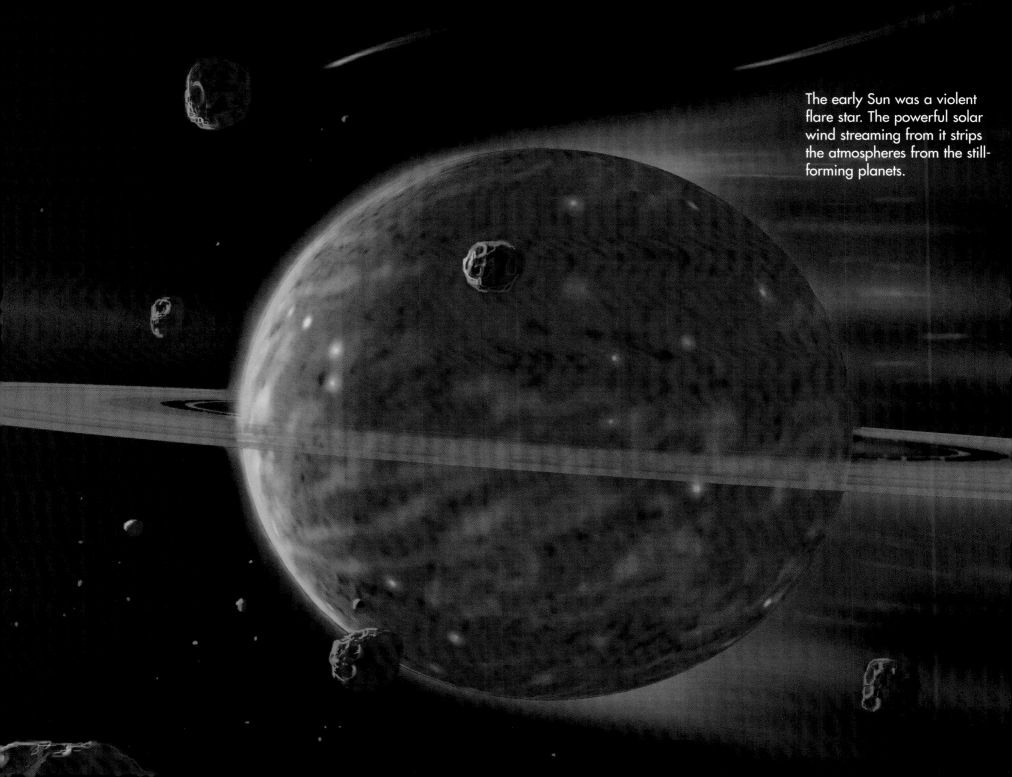

The early Sun was a violent flare star. The powerful solar wind streaming from it strips the atmospheres from the still-forming planets.

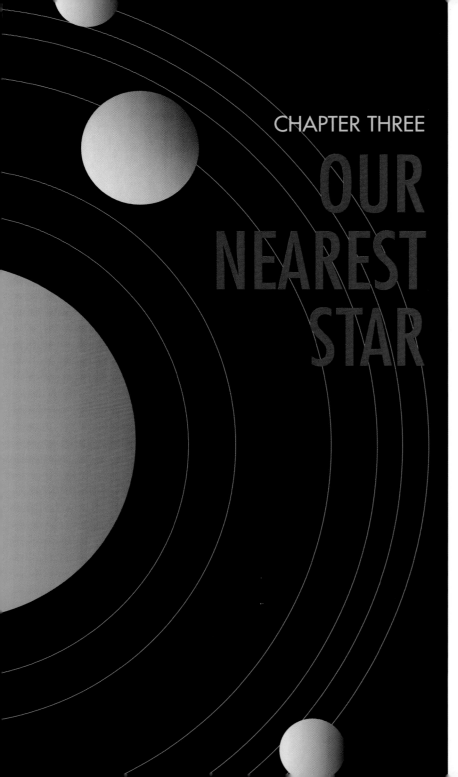

CHAPTER THREE

OUR NEAREST STAR

The Sun is an incandescent ball of gas, one of the 100 billion stars that make up the **Milky Way galaxy**—a vast whirlpooling disk 100,000 **light-years** across. The Sun is located about 30,000 light-years, or two-thirds of the way, from the center of the galaxy. Since it was formed about 5 billion years ago, the Sun has made about 20 trips around the Milky Way, like a rider on a merry-go-round. You might say that the Sun is 20 galaxy years old. Since it is only 93 million miles (150 million km) away (on the average), it is nearer to our planet than any other star—285,000 times closer than the next nearest star. It is a perfectly ordinary star, neither very large nor very small, very hot nor very cool, very young nor very old. It is average in every way.

Average as it is, the Sun still makes our planet seem insignificant. The Sun is nearly 865,000 miles (1,392,000 km) across—more than 100 times greater than Earth. And even though it is made entirely of gas, it weighs 2 billion billion billion tons. More than 1.3 million Earths could fit inside the Sun.

Earth is one member of a family of nine planets that circle the Sun, along with scores of **moons** and thousands of **comets** and **asteroids**. These all formed at about the same time the Sun formed, so all are approximately the same age. Planets are often companions to stars similar to our Sun.

Our galaxy, the Milky Way, is an enormous pinwheel of billions of stars 100,000 light-years across. The Sun and its solar system lies about two-thirds of the way from the center, in one of the spiral arms.

YOU ARE HERE

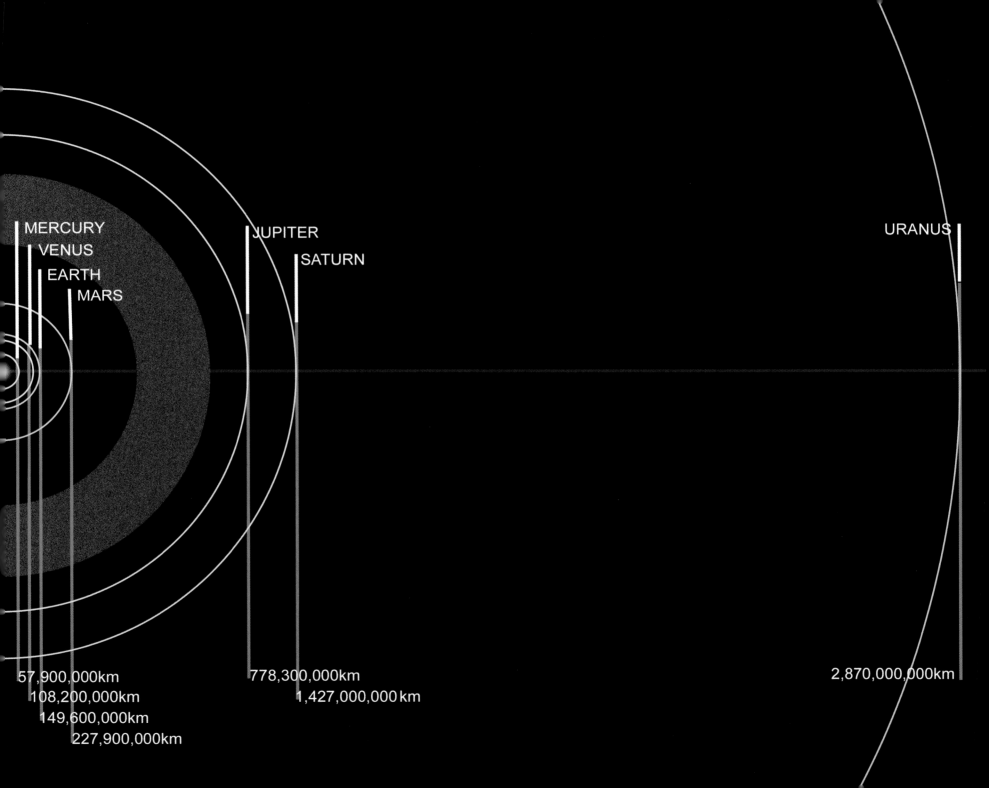

MERCURY

VENUS

EARTH

MARS

JUPITER

SATURN

URANUS

57,900,000km

778,300,000km

2,870,000,000km

108,200,000km

1,427,000,000km

149,600,000km

227,900,000km

NEPTUNE

PLUTO

4,497,000,000km

5,900,000,000km

When two hydrogen atoms collide hard enough they combine, or fuse, into a single atom of helium. This releases energy. It is the fusion of hydrogen into helium that produces all of the energy that comes from the Sun.

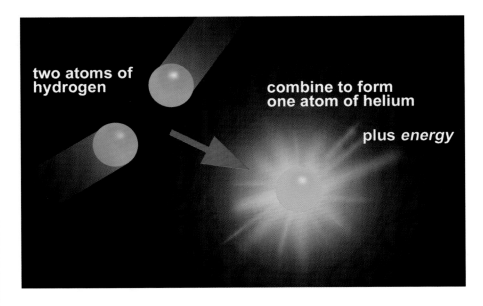

A light-year is the distance a beam of light will travel in one year. Since light travels at the tremendous speed of 186,000 miles (299,000 km) every second, a light-year is a very large distance indeed: nearly 6 trillion miles (9.5 trillion km).

Like most other stars, the Sun gets its energy from fusion, the process of transforming hydrogen into helium. If hydrogen atoms are slammed together hard enough, they form an atom of helium, a slightly heavier element. When this happens, a little bit of the hydrogen is converted into pure energy. This is essentially the same process that occurs in a hydrogen bomb explosion.

The surface temperature of the Sun is an incredible 10,000°F (5,537°C), hot enough to vaporize even the hardest metal. The energy that the Sun emits is equally incredible, the equivalent of 100 gigatons of TNT exploding every second. (One gigaton is a thousand times more powerful than the largest atomic bomb ever detonated.) Yet, pound for pound, your body produces more heat than the Sun. It is only because the Sun is large that it produces so much energy. Dividing the Sun's energy output by its mass shows that it produces about 2 calories a day for every pound. Doing the same for an average human body results in about 10 calories per pound per day—five times the Sun's output!

The Story Told by a Sunbeam

In 1666 Sir Isaac Newton split sunlight into its separate colors by means of a glass prism. The sunlight was spread into a broad band like a rainbow, called a **spectrum**. He proved that white light was really a combination of different colors. In 1802, an English physician named W. H. Wollaston noticed that many fine dark lines crossed the spectrum, but their cause was unknown.

When a substance—solid, liquid, or gas—is heated to incandescence at a high pressure, it gives off a continuous rainbow of colored light, or spectrum. But if a gas is heated at a low pressure, it produces a spectrum composed of isolated bright lines. This is called an **emission spectrum**. Each emission spectrum is unique to the element that produces it, like a fingerprint. For example, the element sodium produces two bright yellow lines in a special position—no other element will do this. Each element and each compound of elements has its own unique color "fingerprint" by which it can be identified. The elements of a light-emitting object can be determined by examining its spectrum.

The mysterious dark lines in the spectrum were explained by G. Kirchhoff in 1859. He found that when light passes through a

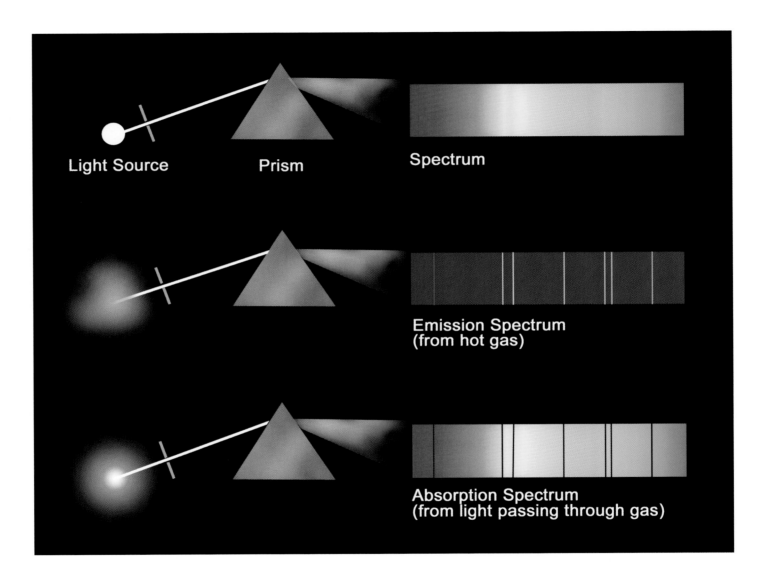

Light Source   Prism   Spectrum

Emission Spectrum
(from hot gas)

Absorption Spectrum
(from light passing through gas)

gas, the gas *absorbs* colors equivalent to the elements that make it up. These absorbed colors leave dark lines in the spectrum. If, for example, white light were to pass through a cloud of sodium gas, the gas would leave dark lines in the spectrum exactly where the yellow lines of glowing sodium would be.

The light from the bright surface of the Sun produces a continuous, unbroken spectrum. But the gases in the atmosphere above the Sun's surface absorb some of this light, according to the elements that the Sun is composed of. This can tell us what elements are in the Sun. When scientists saw, for example, that there were two dark lines exactly where the two yellow lines of sodium would be, they were sure that the element sodium was present. The instrument that astronomers use to study the solar spectrum is called a **spectrograph**. So far, more than 70 different elements have been identified in the solar spectrum, which consists of 76.4 percent hydrogen and 21.8 percent helium. The remaining elements, including oxygen, carbon, neon, and iron, compose less than 1 percent each.

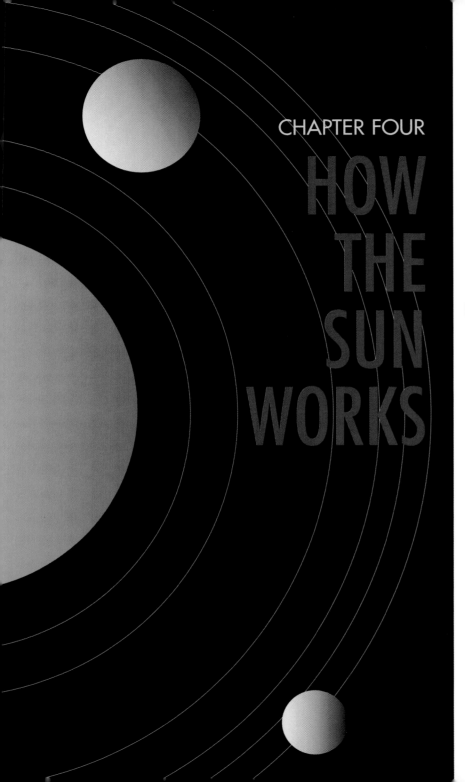

CHAPTER FOUR

HOW THE SUN WORKS

Why is the Sun hot and bright? For most of human history it was assumed that the Sun was burning. No one was able to guess exactly *what* was burning, though. Once people determined how large the Sun is and how the process of combustion works, it was possible to make some guesses.

In 1871 Hermann von Helmholtz, a German scientist, calculated that if the Sun were made of coal it would have to burn 1,500 pounds (680 kilograms) of it every hour on every square foot (0.09 square meter) of its surface. This was clearly impossible—for one thing, the ball of coal would last only a few million years, and the Sun was much older than that—so the Sun had to produce its energy by some other means.

Another theory held that gravitational contraction—the same process that caused the original protostar to heat up—explained the heat, but this did not account for the age of the Sun. For some time it was widely theorized that the heat was produced by the effect of millions upon millions of meteorites falling onto its surface, but this was also soon shown to be just as impossible. Until the 1920s, there was no plausible theory that could account for the heat of the Sun.

(30)

By the first decades of the twentieth century, however, scientists were tracking a new source of energy, one that could produce the kind of energy the Sun created. This was the energy of **nuclear reactions**, a concept first proposed by Sir Arthur Eddington in 1925.

Of the many reactions that take place within the Sun, the most important is called the **solar phoenix reaction**, named after the mythical bird reborn out of fire. This is a three-part fusion reaction in which four hydrogen atoms are combined into a single atom of helium. The total amount of mass left at the end of this combination is slightly less than the mass of the four hydrogen atoms at the beginning—this is where the Sun's light and heat comes from. The missing mass is converted into pure energy. It doesn't take much, either. Of every 2.2 pounds (1 kg) of hydrogen converted into helium, 0.015 pound (0.007 kg) is converted into energy—enough to burn 10 trillion 40-watt light-bulbs.

In three days Earth receives as much energy from the Sun as would be created by burning all the oil and coal reserves *and* all the forests. Yet Earth is so small that it intercepts only one two-billionth of the energy the Sun radiates into space. This unimaginable amount of energy is produced by the conversion of 650 million tons of hydrogen into 645.5 tons of helium every *second*. The difference of 4.55 million tons is converted into pure energy that is ultimately radiated into space and lost forever. This is a huge amount, and it would seem at first that at that rate the Sun would soon run out of fuel. Fortunately, the Sun has 100 billion

billion times the amount of hydrogen it uses every second, so there is plenty left. To date the Sun has used only about half of the hydrogen it possessed when it was born 5 billion years ago.

Inside the Sun

The core of the Sun is an unimaginably fearsome place. Its temperature is 15 million°F (8.3 million°C). This is the temperature at which fusion energy is created under a pressure equal to 250 billion times that of the air pressure at the surface of Earth—3,500 billion pounds per square inch (247 billion kg per square centimeter). This pressure compresses the gas at the core to a density 20 times that of iron. A cubic inch (16.4 cubic centimeters) of this gas would weigh nearly 6 pounds (2.7 kg). The core of the Sun, which accounts for only 1.6 percent of its volume, contains half of the Sun's mass and accounts for 99 percent of all the energy produced.

Its heat travels toward the surface of the Sun by a process called **radiation**, which works in exactly the same way that the heat from a lightbulb disperses from its hot filament. Near the surface of the Sun, the heat has lost some of its energy, and much of it now travels by **convection**. Huge, hot "cells" of gas rise to the surface and sink again. If you watch oatmeal cooking, you can see a similar process taking place. The cells of gas on the Sun are comparable to the clouds over Earth, though thousands of times larger. Many thousands of these rising cells give the visible surface of the Sun a mottled appearance called **granulation**.

The energy coming from the core of the Sun heats the **photosphere**, a layer about 250 miles (400 km) thick. This hot

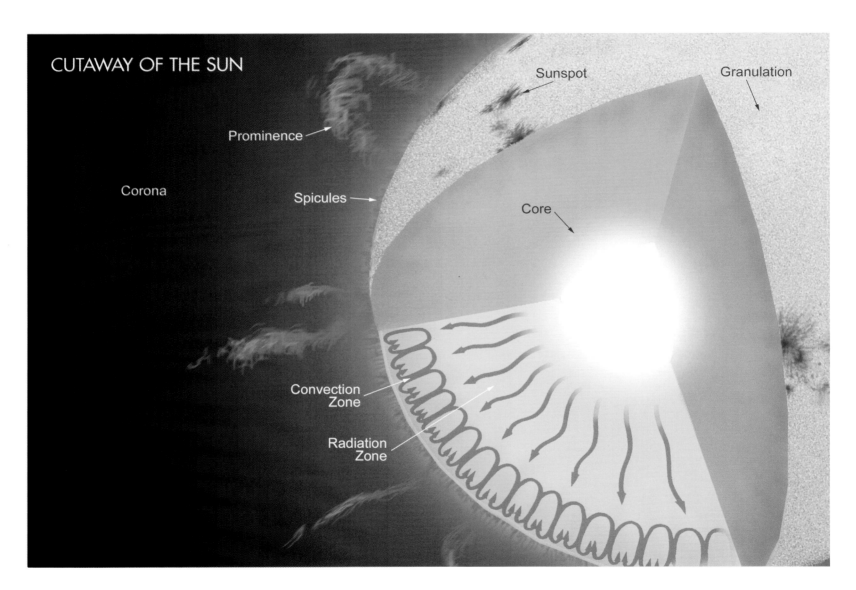

CUTAWAY OF THE SUN

Sunspot

Granulation

Prominence

Corona

Spicules

Core

Convection Zone

Radiation Zone

(34)

"surface" of the Sun produces the light visible to us. (The Sun does not have an actual surface, because it is made entirely of gas.) The temperature here is about 8,300°F (4,600°C). Cells are 600 to 1,200 miles (1,000 to 2,000 km) wide. Between the bright cells are darker regions, where the cooling gas is sinking back into the Sun. Sharp, flamelike jets of gas, called **spicules**, shoot into the **chromosphere**, a glowing layer of gas 1,553 miles (2,500 km) thick.

The chromosphere is normally invisible to the naked eye— covered by the glare of the photosphere—but it becomes visible when the main body of the Sun is covered up, as it is during a **total eclipse**. Above the chromosphere is the **corona**, a region of hot, thin gas that might be considered the Sun's "atmosphere." During an eclipse, the corona is visible as a cloud of pale pink streamers surrounding the Sun. The corona does not have an actual top—it extends outward, growing ever thinner, until it merges with the vacuum of space. The particles that make up the corona move away from the Sun at a speed of 500 miles (800 km) per second in a constant flow called the **solar wind**.

The surface of the Sun is not a peaceful place. Enormous flames, called **prominences**, erupt from the chromosphere. Some of them are far larger than Earth. Some prominences blast away from the Sun at speeds of more than 600 miles (970 km) per second, while others linger like flaming curtains above its surface for hours or days.

The largest eruptions are called **flares**. Flares are caused by **sunspots**, dark whirlpools of magnetic disturbance about one

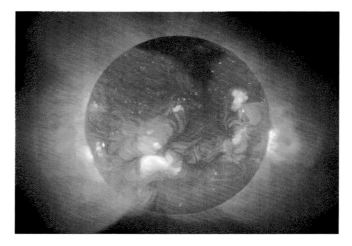

The solar corona is visible in this image taken by an X-ray telescope aboard the Skylab space station in the early 1970s. [NASA/Marshall Space Flight Center Solar Physics Branch]

(36)

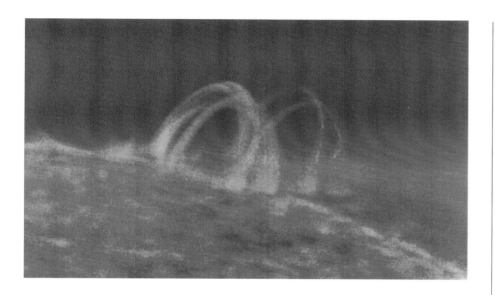

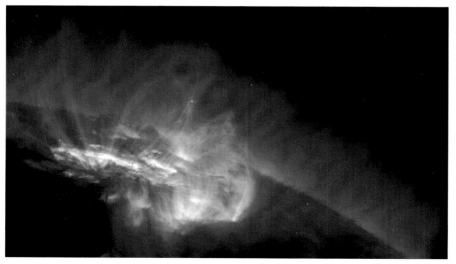

Opposite page: Giant loops of glowing gas follow the lines of magnetic force, rising hundreds of thousands of miles above the surface of the Sun before falling back again. [NASA/TRACE]

Top left: By recording wavelengths of light invisible to the naked eye, special instruments can photograph details in features such as this prominence erupting high above the surface of the Sun. [NASA/TRACE]

Bottom left: Looping magnetic fields are visible in this image of the Sun's surface taken in ultraviolet light by a NASA satellite. [NASA/TRACE]

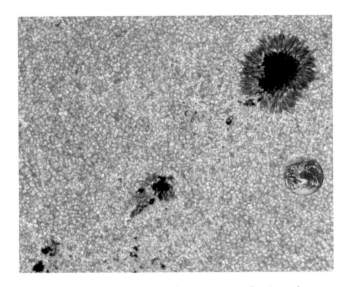

Earth, which is 8,000 miles (12,900 km) wide, compared to a typical sunspot [Lunar and Planetary Institute]

thousand degrees cooler than the surrounding gas. Sunspots seem darker only because they are cooler than the area around them. They still have temperatures of more than 4,000°F (2,200°C), enough to bring most substances to a white heat. Even the smallest sunspot is large enough to swallow the entire Earth, while the biggest ones range up to 80,000 miles (130,000 km) across—ten times larger than our planet.

Sunspots are usually too small to be observed, except through specially equipped telescopes. Occasionally one is large enough to be seen with the naked eye when the Sun is dimmed by misty clouds. Chinese astronomers observed them as early as 600 B.C. In the first half of the nineteenth century, a German astronomer named Heinrich Schwabe discovered that sunspots occur in cycles, with the largest number appearing every 11 years. At the same time, prominences, flares, and solar storms also reach a peak and the furious Sun becomes even more violent than ever.

Sunspots and solar storms have a great impact on Earth. Radiation from the Sun is always pouring down. Most of it is prevented from reaching the surface by Earth's atmosphere and magnetic field. But if a solar storm is strong enough—as happened in early 2001—radiation can penetrate our natural shields. When the Sun is at a peak in its sunspot cycle, solar radiation can seriously disrupt radio, television, and other electronics.

The solar radiation we are most familiar with is, of course, visible light, but there are many other types of radiation we receive as well. **Infrared**, **ultraviolet**, and **X rays** are invisible forms of light. Although we cannot see infrared light, we can feel it in the form of heat. In small doses, ultraviolet light can tan a sunbather's

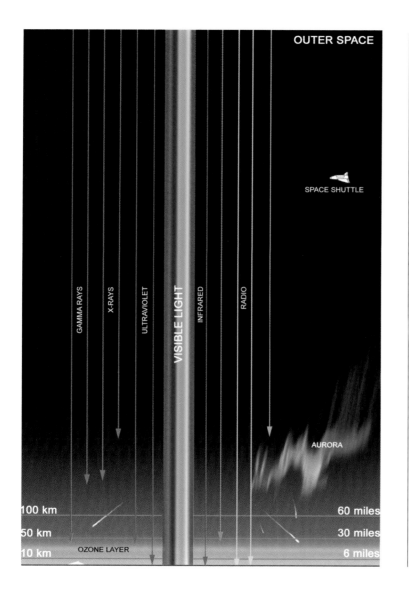

OUTER SPACE

GAMMA RAYS

X-RAYS

ULTRAVIOLET

VISIBLE LIGHT

INFRARED

RADIO

SPACE SHUTTLE

AURORA

100 km

50 km

10 km

OZONE LAYER

60 miles

30 miles

6 miles

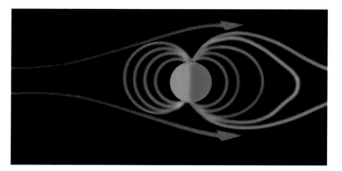

Earth is surrounded by a magnetic field that protects it from the intense radiation of the solar wind. As the energetic particles of the wind spiral down into the polar regions, they collide with the atoms in the upper atmosphere. These glow brightly, and the result is an aurora.

Even though Earth's atmosphere is a fragile barrier—hardly thicker in relation to our planet than the skin of a balloon—it shields us from the most dangerous radiation from the Sun. The ozone layer filters out most of the harmful ultraviolet light. (The small white triangle at the bottom left is Mt. Everest, the world's highest mountain.)

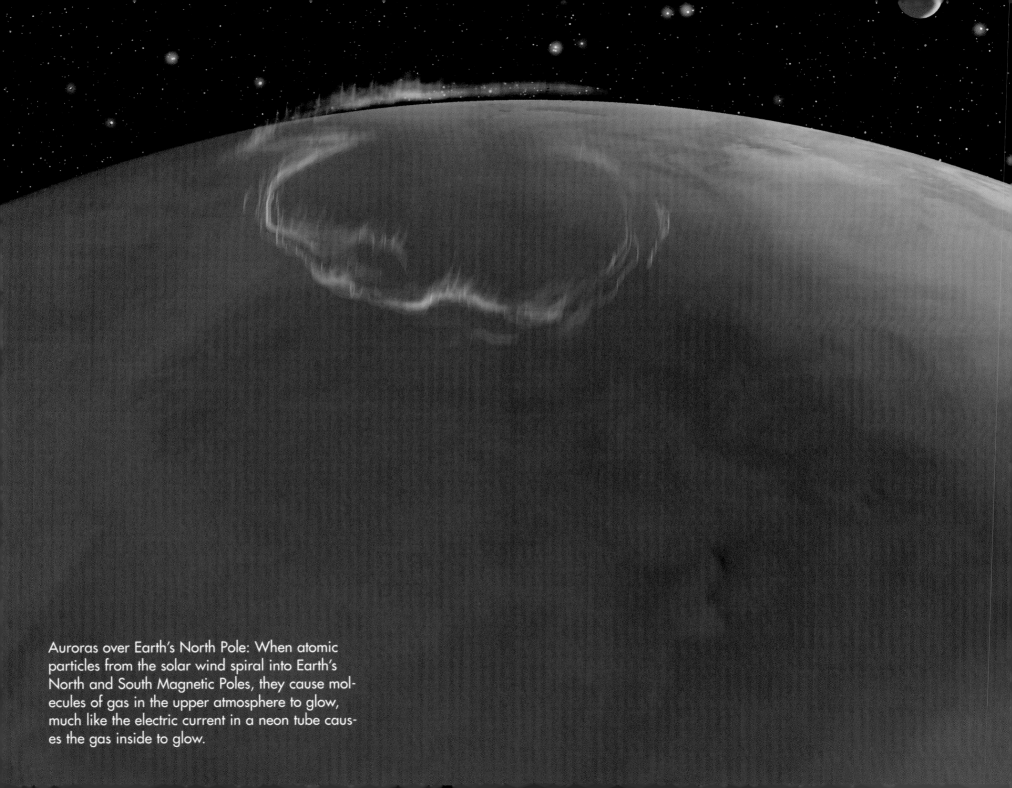

Auroras over Earth's North Pole: When atomic particles from the solar wind spiral into Earth's North and South Magnetic Poles, they cause molecules of gas in the upper atmosphere to glow, much like the electric current in a neon tube causes the gas inside to glow.

skin, but too much can cause serious burns and even cancer. It is not at all inaccurate to describe a sunburn as a first-degree radiation burn.

In addition to radiation, solar flares emit streams of atomic particles, such as electrons and protons, that are blasted outward from the Sun in a solar wind that reaches as far as the orbit of Saturn. As these particles rush past Earth, they are attracted by the North and South Magnetic Poles, like iron filings gathering around the ends of a magnet. When the particles spiral into the upper atmosphere, they strike molecules of gas and cause them to glow, much as electricity passing through the gas in a neon tube causes it to glow. We see this glowing gas as swirling rays and curtains of colored light, which is called an **aurora**. During the great solar storm of early 2001, auroras were seen as far south as Texas.

The southern lights (aurora australis) as seen from the space shuttle in 1991. The aurora australis appears above Earth's South Pole just as the northern lights, or aurora borealis, appear above the North Pole. They range from 50 to 60 miles (80 to 96 km) above the surface. The tail of the space shuttle is surrounded by glowing ionized gas, similar to the aurora itself. [NASA]

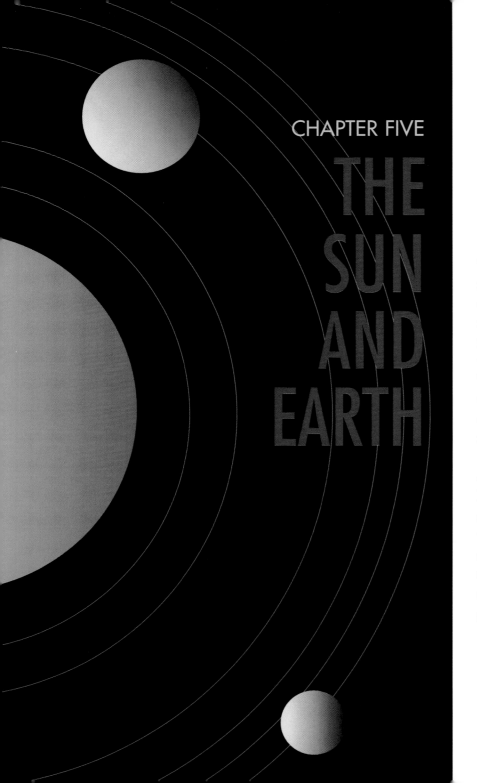

CHAPTER FIVE

THE SUN AND EARTH

The Sun interacts with Earth in many ways. Its light and warmth make life possible on our planet. Although, at the same time, it emits radiation that would be deadly to life on Earth if it were not for the shielding effect of our atmosphere and our magnetic field. Ultraviolet is the most dangerous. It is so powerful that it's used in laboratories and hospitals to sterilize tools and equipment. The solar wind would be deadly, too, if it were able to penetrate to Earth's surface. But the gases in our atmosphere filter out many of the Sun's harmful rays, while our magnetic field deflects other rays like a shield, which causes them to bend around Earth.

Fortunately, Earth's atmosphere is quite effective at filtering out harmful radiation, while at the same time permitting light and heat to reach its surface. Less appreciated, but just as fortunate, the atmosphere also lets this heat *escape*. The infrared radiation that warms the surface of Earth is powerful enough to penetrate the atmosphere. But the infrared radiation that the warm surface radiates back toward space is weaker and has a much harder time penetrating clouds and the like. This is exactly how a greenhouse for growing plants works.

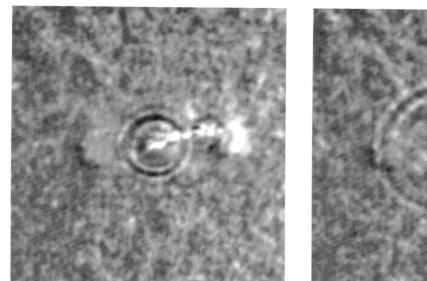 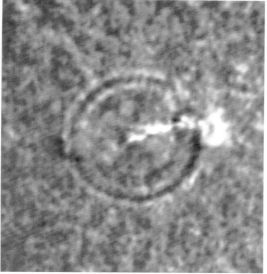 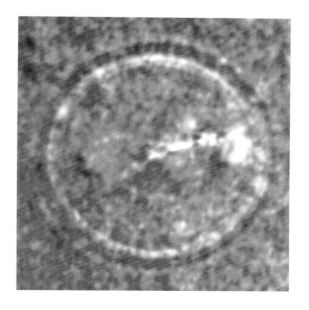

If Earth were to be completely covered by clouds, or a layer of something like carbon dioxide, the heat from the Sun would be unable to get back out again. It would be trapped beneath the clouds. In such a case, Earth would grow warmer and warmer, until it became too hot to support life. This is called the **greenhouse effect**. It has already happened on the planet Venus, which closely resembles Earth in many ways. Its dense blanket of carbon dioxide clouds has held heat and created a greenhouse effect that has driven the surface temperature of Venus to more than 1,000°F (600°C)—hot enough to melt tin or lead.

A sunquake was observed by a NASA satellite in 1996. The eruption of a flare set off waves on the surface of the Sun like those caused by a rock dropped into a pond. Starting off with a speed of 22,000 miles (35,400 km) per hour, the waves eventually reached a speed of 250,000 miles (402,250 km) per hour. [NASA/SOHO]

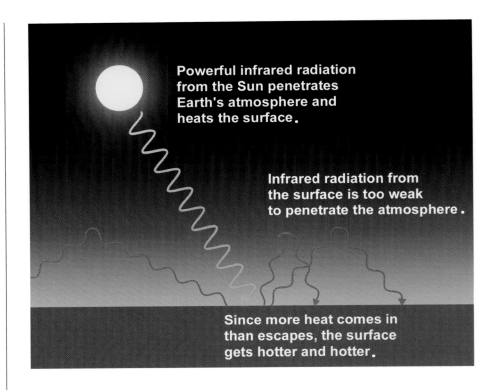

Powerful infrared radiation from the Sun penetrates Earth's atmosphere and heats the surface.

Infrared radiation from the surface is too weak to penetrate the atmosphere.

Since more heat comes in than escapes, the surface gets hotter and hotter.

Solar radiation causes the oxygen molecules in the upper atmosphere to form **ozone**. Any kind of energy—for example, lightning or electronic devices—can create ozone from ordinary oxygen. The crisp smell after an electrical storm, or the distinctive odor from electrical equipment, is given off by ozone. In very small quantities it smells fresh and pleasant and is harmless, but in large quantities it is poisonous.

Fortunately, the ozone that the Sun's energy creates is located in a layer 20 to 60 miles (30 to 100 km) above the surface of Earth. There it serves a useful purpose: It helps screen the surface of our planet from ultraviolet radiation. It would be difficult to sustain life on Earth if not for this screen. Mars, for example, has no way of filtering out ultraviolet light, and many scientists think that this may have prevented life from becoming established there.

The **ozone layer** is fragile, however, and certain chemicals can destroy it. Some of the gases once used in spray cans were harmful to it, for example, but now their use is prohibited. Still, there are disturbing signs that all is not well with our ozone layer. Scientists have found large "holes" in it—places where the ozone is very thin, allowing too much dangerous ultraviolet light through to Earth's surface. The ultraviolet energy from the Sun is responsible for many types of skin cancer, so people need to be even more careful than usual about Sun exposure where the ozone layer is thin.

Making the Sun Work for Us

Although it can be dangerous, the radiation from the Sun is very useful. More than two thousand years ago, the Greek engineer and mathematician Archimedes discovered that the Sun's rays could be focused by the use of mirrors or reflectors, creating an enormous amount of heat. It is said that he used this invention as a kind of heat ray to destroy enemy ships.

In the nineteenth century several inventors discovered that if the Sun's heat were focused on a boiler, it could generate steam

Huge solar panels convert sunlight into electrical power for the International Space Station. [NASA]

that would run an engine. Eventually it was found that certain materials, when exposed to sunlight, could generate an electrical current. The current was weak, but if enough of these "solar cells" or "solar batteries" were hooked together, large amounts of electrical energy could be produced. (Small solar cells can power a pocket calculator.) Solar cells are one of the most important sources of energy in space flight. The enormous, glittering, purplish-blue "wings" on the International Space Station are giant panels of solar cells.

Operators of plant nurseries have learned to make good use of the greenhouse effect. They construct large buildings entirely of glass, where they can keep the interior warm enough to grow flowers and vegetables during even the coldest winter. The energy from the Sun easily penetrates the glass and warms the soil underneath, but the radiation coming from the warm soil is too weak to pass back out through the glass. More heat is coming in than is escaping, so the greenhouse remains nice and warm.

Eclipses

Every now and then we are able to enjoy a magnificent event. The sky grows dark and stars can be seen in the middle of the day. It becomes chilly and gloomy. Birds stop singing because it seems that night has fallen. The Sun now looks like a dark circle surrounded by an eerily glowing halo.

Eclipses have been observed since ancient times, though their cause was unknown. Some of the earliest written accounts are by ancient Chinese astronomers. Eclipses were awesome events that

When the Moon passes in front of the Sun, it causes a solar eclipse, allowing us to see the beautiful corona that surrounds our star.

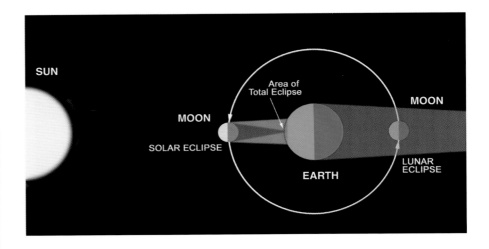

some thought foretold great evil. But by the sixth century B.C., Greek scientists had figured out what produced them. It was nothing more than the Moon passing in front of the Sun.

The Moon and the Sun appear to be almost exactly the same size in the sky. Because the Moon orbits Earth while Earth revolves around the Sun, there are occasions when the Moon passes directly between Earth and the Sun. The Moon's orbit is tipped slightly, so this doesn't happen every time the Moon goes around Earth. (Otherwise, we'd have an eclipse every month.) When the alignment is perfect, the result is a total eclipse, but if the Moon slightly misses covering the Sun completely, the result is a **partial eclipse**. During a total eclipse, the moon covers the brilliant solar disk and the Sun's glowing atmosphere becomes visible to the naked eye.

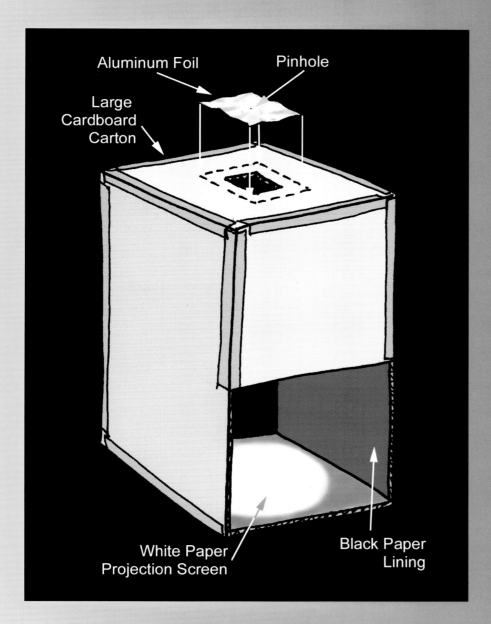

Aluminum Foil

Pinhole

Large Cardboard Carton

White Paper Projection Screen

Black Paper Lining

NEVER try to observe the Sun with your naked eyes. ABSOLUTELY NEVER attempt to observe the Sun with binoculars or a telescope. The accumulated heat and light focused into your eye can permanently blind you.

Take a magnifying glass outside on a sunny day, and focus the sunlight onto a piece of paper. It takes only a second or two for a smoldering brown spot to appear as the concentrated sunlight ignites the paper. That's exactly what a telescope will do to your eye if you use it to look at the Sun.

There are, fortunately, ways that are not only much safer but much *better*. The simplest method is to make a pinhole projector. All you need is a large cardboard carton, some aluminum foil, some tape and scissors, a drawing compass, and white drawing paper. Cut a hole at one end of the box, and tape a square of aluminum foil over it. With the point of the compass, punch a smooth round hole in the center of the foil. On the inside of the box, opposite the pinhole, tape or glue a sheet of white paper or poster board.

Take your projector out on a sunny day and point the end of the box with the pinhole toward the Sun. Turn the box so the inside is shaded, and you'll see a large round circle of light projected onto the white paper. This is an image of the Sun. If there are sunspots, you will be able to see them too. If you trace them onto a piece of paper every day, you'll be able to observe their motion as they rotate with the Sun (the Sun takes 25 days to rotate once). You can also keep track of the number of sunspots and their growth.

The Moon's orbit is also not perfectly circular—it orbits in an **ellipse**. For this reason, the Moon is sometimes closer to Earth than at other times. If an eclipse occurs when the Moon is at its farthest distance from Earth, it doesn't cover the Sun entirely—there is a thin ring of Sun showing all around it. When this happens it is called an **annular eclipse**, or ring-shaped eclipse. Since the moon is in constant motion as it circles Earth, no eclipse lasts longer than about eight minutes, and most are shorter.

Eclipses are very beautiful, awe-inspiring sights, but they are also important for scientists. When they occur, astronomers study the corona, as well as prominences and flares as they erupt past the dark edge of the Moon.

You can draw an ellipse by looping a piece of string around a pair of thumbtacks or pushpins stuck in a drawing board. Put the point of a pencil into the loop and keep the string taut. The points that the tacks mark are called foci (singular *focus*). Different ellipses can be made by moving the tacks closer together or farther apart. The closer they are, the more circular the ellipse will be (in fact, a circle can be considered a special kind of ellipse in which both foci fall on the same point).

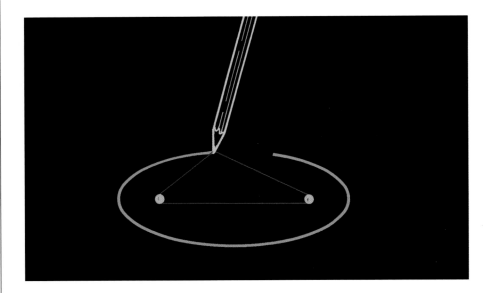

CHAPTER SIX

OUR STAR GROWS OLD

About 1.1 billion years from now, the Sun will begin to change. As the hydrogen fuel in its core is used up, the burning will spread outward toward the surface. This will make the Sun grow brighter, and the increased radiation will have a devastating effect on Earth. After another two to three billion years, the Sun may be twice as bright as it is now. The mean surface temperature of Earth will rise from about 68°F (20°C) to 167°F (75°C). Earth's oceans will evaporate, and the planet will become a stark, lifeless desert. Finally, at the age of almost 11 billion years, the Sun will run out of hydrogen almost entirely.

The helium that has been accumulating in the core since the Sun's creation will become unstable and begin to collapse under its own weight. The core will become even denser and hotter, and the last remaining dregs of hydrogen will squeeze out into a thin shell surrounding the core. Meanwhile, the Sun will swell one-and-a-half times its normal size and grow more than twice as bright. This is how the Sun will enter its old age.

It won't grow any brighter over the next 700 million years, but it will continue to grow larger, swelling to more than twice its present size. As it does so, it will cool down a little. From the

Two or three billion years from now as the Sun grows larger and hotter, Earth's oceans will nearly disappear. What appear to be banks of snow are actually thick layers of salt.

parched surface of Earth, the Sun will appear as an enormous orange ball hanging in the misty sky.

At the age of 11.6 billion years, the Sun will again begin to grow rapidly and at just over 12 billion years it will blow off more than a quarter of the mass of its outer surface. With a less massive Sun to attract them, the planets' orbits will change. Venus will become as distant as Earth is now, and Earth will move even farther away. Eighty-three million years later, the ever-swelling Sun will become a **red giant**. It will become 166 times larger than the Sun we know, almost as large as the present orbit of Earth. The planet Mercury will be devoured in the flames of the swelling Sun. The mountains of Earth will melt and flow like red-hot molasses into vast, flat seas of lava. A bloated red Sun will fill more than half the sky.

As the Sun reaches its maximum size as a red giant, the helium core will reach a temperature of 100 million degrees. This is hot enough to trigger helium fusion, creating a new source of energy. At first it will seem as though the Sun has gotten a new lease on life. It will shrink in size, though never smaller than about ten times its present size. It will begin a period of relative stability that will last for the next 110 million years. All the while, helium fusion will produce carbon and oxygen in the core. As these elements accumulate, new reactions will set in, and the Sun will again begin to swell until it doubles its size. Finally, the core will run out of helium. The carbon and oxygen will collapse, but this will not create enough heat to start carbon fusion. (The Sun isn't massive enough for that to happen.)

Three billion years from now, the Sun will become a sub-giant, two or three times larger than the Sun we know today. Our planet will become a cloud-covered furnace much like Venus is now.

Four billion years from now, the Sun will swell to an enormous size—as large as the orbit of Mercury—as it becomes a red giant. The tremendous heat will melt Earth's surface.

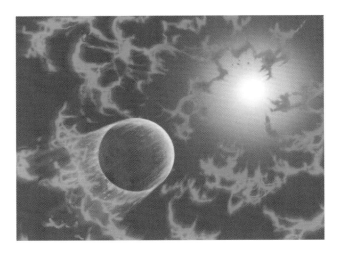

Four and a half billion years from now: the last gasp of the Sun. As the Sun blows off the outer layers of its atmosphere, what remains of Earth is incinerated.

Out of fuel, the Sun will approach the beginning of the end. It will bloat to an enormous size as the last dregs of helium and hydrogen are blown away. It will become 180 times larger than the Sun we know and thousands of times brighter. Huge quantities of its atmosphere will be thrown off into space, until nearly half its mass is lost. The loss of mass will cause the planets Venus and Earth—now little more than cinders—to move even farther away.

The thin shell of helium surrounding the carbon-oxygen core will become unstable, and the Sun will begin to pulse violently. Every 100,000 years it will suddenly balloon to more than 200 times its old size, becoming brighter in the process. And every time it does this, it will lose more mass. A final pulse will blow away the last of the Sun's outer surface. All that will be left is the bare core, a sphere about the size of Earth. This will be extremely hot, but it is just residual heat—nothing will replace it as it is lost. The former Sun, now a **white dwarf**, will begin to cool off, though it will take many billions of years before it loses the last of its heat. That will be all that remains of the Sun, that and an ever-expanding shell of gas, brilliantly glowing from the core's ultraviolet radiation.

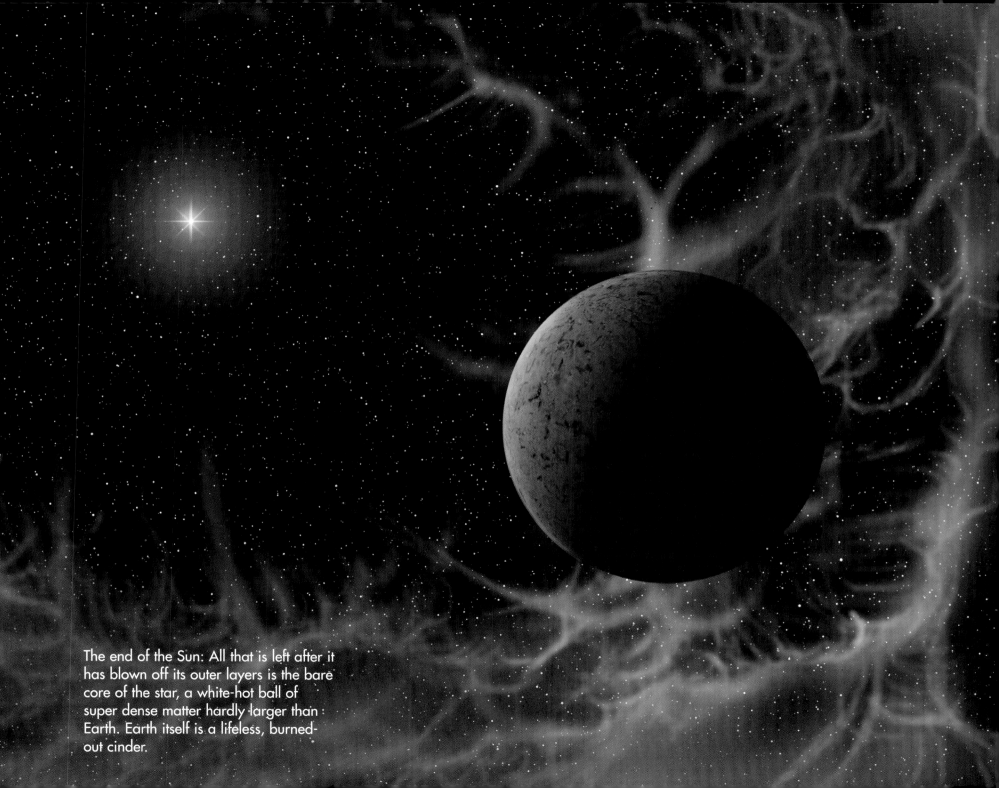

The end of the Sun: All that is left after it has blown off its outer layers is the bare core of the star, a white-hot ball of super dense matter hardly larger than Earth. Earth itself is a lifeless, burned-out cinder.

annular eclipse: an eclipse in which the Moon doesn't quite cover the Sun, leaving a thin ring of light showing all the way around. From the Latin word for "ring."

asteroid: a rocky or metallic interplanetary body, usually more than 328 ft (100 m) in diameter.

atmosphere: a layer of gas surrounding a star or planet.

atom: a particle of matter composed of a nucleus surrounded by orbiting electrons.

aurora: glowing, often moving colored lights seen near the North and South Poles of Earth (and some other plan-

ets), caused by sun radiation colliding with high-altitude air molecules.

centrifugal force: an apparent force that causes matter to move away from the center of rotation.

charged particle: an atomic particle, such as an electron, that carries an electrical charge. Protons carry a positive charge and neutrons have no charge at all.

chromosphere: a reddish layer of the Sun's atmosphere, just above the photosphere.

comet: an icy interplanetary body that, when heated by the Sun as it enters the inner

solar system, releases gases that form a bright head and long glowing tail.

convection: a way in which heat moves from a hot area to a cold one—the heat is carried by the motion of the heated material itself.

core: the densest inner region of a star, planet, or other object. In planets, the core is often rocky or metallic. In stars it is the dense central region where nuclear reactions occur.

corona: the outmost layer of the Sun's atmosphere. From the Latin word for "crown."

dwarf star: a star smaller than the average size.

eclipse: an event when the shadow of one body falls onto another.

electron: one of the negatively charged particles that orbit the nucleus of an atom.

ellipse: a shape like a flattened circle or oval.

emission spectrum: the spectrum created by hot gases.

energy: in physics, energy refers to a quality equal to a certain amount of work. It may take the form of light, heat, or motion.

flare: a sudden, short-lived burst of energy from the Sun that can eject gas at high speeds.

fusion: the process by which light hydrogen atoms are forced together to form heavier helium atoms. When this happens, some of the mass of the hydrogen is converted into pure energy.

granulation: the visible effect of heat cells rising to the surface of the Sun.

greenhouse effect: the heating of a planet's atmosphere by the absorption of heat radiated from its surface.

helium: the second-lightest element (after hydrogen). It is the product of nuclear fusion.

hydrogen: the lightest and most common element in the universe.

infrared radiation: light radiation with a wavelength too long to see.

ion: an electrically charged atom or molecule.

ionization: the process of creating electrically charged atoms or molecules.

light-year: the distance that light travels in one year—approximately 6 trillion miles (9.5 trillion km).

Milky Way galaxy: the galaxy of which our Sun and solar system are a part.

molecule: a combination of two or more atoms.

moon: any body orbiting around a planet.

nebula: a dense cloud of dark or glowing gas in open space or surrounding a star. From the Latin word for "cloud."

nuclear reaction: a reaction that involves the nucleus of an atom changing its mass.

nucleus (plural *nuclei*): the matter at the center of an atom, composed of protons and neutrons.

ozone: a special form of oxygen molecule. Molecules of ordinary oxygen are composed of two atoms of oxygen (O_2), while ozone is made of three oxygen atoms (O_3).

ozone layer: a layer of ozone created by solar radiation that lies 20 to 60 miles (30 to 100 km) above the surface of Earth.

partial eclipse: an eclipse in which the Moon covers only part of the Sun.

photosphere: the layer of the Sun that emits visible light. From Latin words meaning "sphere of light."

photosynthesis: the chemical process by which plants use the energy from the Sun to create their food. From the Greek word meaning "creating with light."

prominence: a large cloud or jet of gas blown from the surface of the Sun into the surrounding corona.

protostar: a cloud of gas and dust contracting into the dense mass that will eventually form a main-sequence star.

radiation: any of the various kinds of electromagnetic waves or atomic particles that transmit energy across space, such as light, radio, X rays, etc.

red giant: an old main-sequence star whose surface layers have expanded enormously.

solar phoenix reaction: the process by which the Sun creates its energy by fusing hydrogen atoms into helium atoms. Some of the mass of the hydrogen atom is converted into pure energy, creating the Sun's light and heat.

solar wind: the outrushing gas from the Sun that reaches as far as Earth and even beyond the outer planets.

solstice: the winter solstice, which usually falls on or near December 22, marks the beginning of winter in the Northern Hemisphere when daylight is shortest. The summer solstice, which falls on or near June 22, occurs on the first day of summer in the Northern Hemisphere when daylight is longest.

spectrograph: an instrument that breaks light into its spectrum and records the results.

spectrum: the rainbow-colored band formed when light passes through a prism.

spicule: a very narrow, short-lived jet of gas shooting out from the chromosphere.

star: a mass of gaseous material large enough to trigger nuclear reactions in its core.

sunspot: a magnetic storm on the surface of the Sun that is cooler than its surrounding area.

supernova: a star that explodes with tremendous force, blowing off most of its mass and leaving only its dense core behind.

total eclipse: when the Moon covers the whole Sun, leaving only the corona visible.

ultraviolet radiation: light radiation with a wavelength that is too short to see.

vacuum: the absence of matter; empty space.

white dwarf: a star with a mass about the same as that of our Sun but only about the size of Earth. It is one of the final stages of a dying star.

x-ray radiation: Very high-energy electromagnetic radiation that is more powerful than ultraviolet radiation and would be very dangerous to life if Earth's atmospere didn't filter out most of it.

yellow dwarf: a star slightly smaller than average. Our Sun is a yellow dwarf, so-called because yellow is the dominant color in its spectrum.

Online

Live from the Sun
http://www.fsus.fsu.edu/
mcquone/InvestUniv/LvfromSn
.htm
An excellent source of information about the Sun, with links to many related Web sites.

NASA Spacelink
http://spacelink.msfc.nasa.gov/
index.html
Gateway to many NASA Web sites about the Sun and planets.

Nine Planets
http://www.nineplanets.org
Detailed information about the Sun, the planets, and all the moons, including many photos and useful links to other Web sites.

Planet Orbits
http://www.alcyone.de
A free software program that allows the user to see the positions of all the planets in the solar system at one time.

Planet's Visibility
http://www.alcyone.de
A free software program that allows users to find out when they can see a particular planet and where to look for it in the sky.

Solar System Simulator
http://space.jpl.nasa.gov/
An amazing Web site that allows the visitor to travel to all the planets and moons and create their own views of these distant worlds.

Books

Beatty, J. Kelly, Carolyn Collins Petersen and Andrew Chaikin, eds. *The New Solar System*. Cambridge, MA: Sky Publishing Corp, 1999.

Branley, Franklyn M. *The Sun and the Solar System*. Brookfield, CT: Twenty-First Century Books, 1996.

Clay, Rebecca. *Stars and Galaxies*. Brookfield, CT: Twenty-First Century Books, 1997.

Hartmann, William K. *Moons and Planets*. Belmont, CA: Wadsworth Publishing Co., 1999.

Kallen, Stuart A. *Exploring the Origins of the Universe*. Brookfield, CT: Twenty-First Century Books, 1997.

Miller, Ron, and William K. Hartmann. *The Grand Tour*. New York: Workman Publishing Co., 1993.

Scagell, Robine. *The New Book of Space*. Brookfield, CT: Copper Beech, 1997.

Schaaf, Fred. *Planetology*. Danbury, CT: Franklin Watts, 1996.

Vogt, Gregory L. *Deep Space Astronomy*. Brookfield, CT: Twenty-First Century Books, 1999.

Magazines

Sky & Telescope
http://www.skypub.com

Astronomy
http://www.astronomy.com

Organizations

American Astronomical Society
2000 Florida Avenue NW,
Suite 400
Washington, DC 20009-1231
http://www.AAS.org

Association of Lunar and Planetary
  Observers
P.O. Box 171302
Memphis, TN 38187-1302
http://www.lpl.arizona.edu/alpo/

Astronomical Society of the Pacific
390 Ashton Avenue
San Francisco, CA 94112
http://www.apsky.org

The Planetary Society
65 N. Catalina Avenue
Pasadena, CA 91106
http://planetary.org